GRAPHIC MYTHOLOGY

MESOAMERICAN MYTHS

by David West

illustrated by Mike Taylor

The Rosen Publishing Group, Inc., New York

Published in 2006 by The Rosen Publishing Group, Inc.
29 East 21st Street, New York, NY 10010

First edition, 2006

Designed and produced by
David West Books

Editor: Dominique Crowley

Photo credits:
Pages 4, Jack Poe
Page 5, Skip Hunt

Library of Congress Cataloging-in-Publication Data

West, David
  Mesoamerican myths / by David West ; illustrated by Mike Taylor.
     p. cm. — (Graphic mythology)
  Includes bibliographical references and index.
  ISBN 1-4042-0802-X (lib. bdg. : alk. paper) — ISBN 1-4042-0814-3 (pbk. : alk.
paper) — ISBN 1-4042-6254-7 (6 pack : alk. paper)
  1. Aztec mythology. 2. Maya mythology. 3. Indian mythology — Mexico. I. Title.
II. Series.
  F1219.3.R3.W47 2005
  299.7'8452—dc22

                                    2005018266

Manufactured in China

CONTENTS

ANCIENT CIVILIZATIONS

Mesoamerica, the name used to describe Mexico and Central America, has a rich history of ancient cultures and civilizations. The Toltecs were one of the earliest cultures, and many of their gods influenced the later civilizations of the Maya and the Aztecs.

RELIGION AND MYTHOLOGY

Religion and mythology were central to the lives of these ancient cultures. Myths, and stories about gods, helped them make sense of the world. The Aztecs, for example, believed that the Spanish explorer Hernan Cortés, who conquered them, was not a foreign enemy, but the returning god, Quetzalcóatl.

Aztecs believed that the world was created five times. On the calendar above, the four rectangles around the central sun god represent the four previous creations of life on Earth.

This Mayan statue of a tlachtli player looks out over the jungle. Tlachtli was a sacred ball-game played by Mesoamericans. In the game, two teams tried to bounce a rubber ball through a stone hoop high up on a wall.

A sculptured reptile sticks out from Teotihuacán's Temple of Quetzalcóatl (right). Often, these sculptures were painted in bright colors, and the eyes were made of volcanic glass.

HEAVENS ABOVE

Mesoamerican cultures believed that there was not just one heaven, but many. One way to reach these heavens was by human sacrifice. People were willing to be killed because they hoped that they would go to heaven. Sacrifice was a horrible way to die, and often the heart was ripped out of the body. Another reason people were sacrificed was to honor the gods, and to ensure healthy crops. Hell, on the other hand, was not a scary, hot furnace, but a place of emptiness and boredom.

Sacrifice was common to all the Mesoamerican cultures. Some myths are stories that give reasons for these killings.

THREE MESOAMERICAN MYTHS

Mesoamerica was an area that included Mexico and Central America before parts of it were taken over in the sixteenth century by Europeans. It was home to the Toltec, Olmec, Aztec, and Mayan civilizations. By reading the myths, we can learn a lot about these cultures.

QUETZALCÓATL AND TEZCATLIPOCA CREATE THE WORLD (AZTEC)

The Aztecs believed that the world was created five times. The gods kept destroying the world because they were not pleased with what they had made. Each time they re-created it, they tried to make the world better. This myth is the story of the fifth, and final, creation. It tells of what happened when two gods, Quetzalcóatl and Tezcatlipoca, destroyed the goddess Tlatecuhtli and used her body to create the world for the last time.

Quetzalcóatl
A very important god in Aztec mythology, this feathered snake shares his name with a famous king from the Toltec civilization. He is a kind god. In human form, he has a gray beard.

Tezcatlipoca
The god of warriors, the night sky, and the thunderbolt, he is also known as the Smoking Mirror because he carries a magic mirror. This mirror shows people's thoughts.

Tlatecuhtli
Sometimes known as the Earth Monster, this goddess lives in water. Some say that 20,000 people every year are sacrificed by the Aztecs to please her.

CREATION OF THE SUN, MOON, AND PEOPLE (AZTEC)

Creation stories help people understand who they are and why they are alive. They provide important links to a long-lost past, especially to the way of life of their ancestors. This creation story helped Aztecs imagine how the world might have begun. It contains information about the gods, sacrifice, and religion, and shows that people cannot be judged by their appearance.

Tecciztécatl
This god of snails is proud and attractive. Later, he becomes the god of the moon.

Nanautzin
Known as the Scabby One, Nanautzin is small, quiet, and thoughtful. He always wears old clothes.

Mictlantecuhtli
This god of the dead lives in the underworld, a place where evil spirits go after death.

THE HERO TWINS (MAYA)

According to the Popol Vuh and Mayan mythology, there were two sets of hero twins. Both enjoyed the sacred ball-game, tlachtli, but they played it so noisily that they upset the gods. The lords of the underworld challenged them to a game of ball, with a fatal outcome.

Hun Hunahpu
Vucub Hunahpu's twin, this forefather god has four sons.

Vucub Hunahpu
The other hero twin, he has neither a wife nor children.

Hun Came
One of two Kings of Death. He rules the underworld (Xibalba).

Vucub Came
The other Lord of the underworld. His Mayan name means Seven Death.

Hunahpu
Son of Hun Hunahpu, and the hero twin brother of Xbalanque.

Xbalanque
Clever hero twin. He uses great skill when playing ball in the underworld.

QUETZALCÓATL AND TEZCATLIPOCA CREATE THE WORLD
FROM THE AZTEC PEOPLE

HUH! WHAT IS THAT?

TWO OF THE MANY GODS HAVE BEEN CREATING PARTS OF THE WORLD. QUETZALCÓATL, THE FEATHERED SERPENT GOD, AND TEZCATLIPOCA, GOD OF THE SMOKING MIRROR, LOOK DOWN ON THE WATER FROM THE SKY.

IT IS TLATECUHTLI, THE GIANT WATER GODDESS. AND SHE'S EATING EVERYTHING WE HAVE CREATED!

THE GODDESS EATS WHILE THE TWO GODS DECIDE WHAT TO DO...

LET US JOIN FORCES TO RID OURSELVES OF THIS MONSTER.

YES, CHANGE INTO A SNAKE. SNAKES FIGHT BETTER IN WATER...

THEY DIVE OUT OF THE CLOUDS...

...INTO THE OCEAN...

...AND SNEAK UP TO TLATECUHTLI FROM BELOW.

QUETZALCÓATL GRABS THE GODDESS BY THE ARMS...

TEZCATLIPOCA GRABS HER BY THE LEGS...

BEFORE SHE CAN DEFEND HERSELF, TLATECUHTLI IS PULLED APART...

...AND THE BROKEN PIECES OF HER BODY BECOME THE EARTH.

WHEN THE OTHER GODS HEAR WHAT HAS HAPPENED, THEY ARE VERY ANGRY.

TO PLEASE TLATECUHTLI, SHE SHALL HAVE THE HONOR OF PROVIDING FOR ALL LIVING THINGS.

FROM HER HAIR, THEY CREATE TREES, GRASS, AND FLOWERS...

CAVES, FOUNTAINS, AND WELLS FROM HER EYES...

11

RIVERS FROM HER MOUTH...

AND MOUNTAINS FROM HER SHOULDERS.

BUT TLATECUHTLI IS UNHAPPY. WHEN PEOPLE APPEAR IN THE WORLD, THEY CAN HEAR HER CRYING IN THE NIGHT.

AAAIIEEE

THEY KNOW SHE IS THIRSTY FOR THEIR BLOOD.

SHE WILL NOT PROVIDE FOOD FROM THE SOIL UNTIL SHE DRINKS BLOOD!

AND SO...

SHE WHO PROVIDES FOR HUMAN LIVES...

DEMANDS HUMAN LIVES TO PROVIDE FOR HER!

SO IT HAS ALWAYS BEEN, SO IT WILL BE FOREVER.

THE END

13

THE CREATION OF
THE SUN, MOON, AND PEOPLE
FROM THE AZTEC PEOPLE

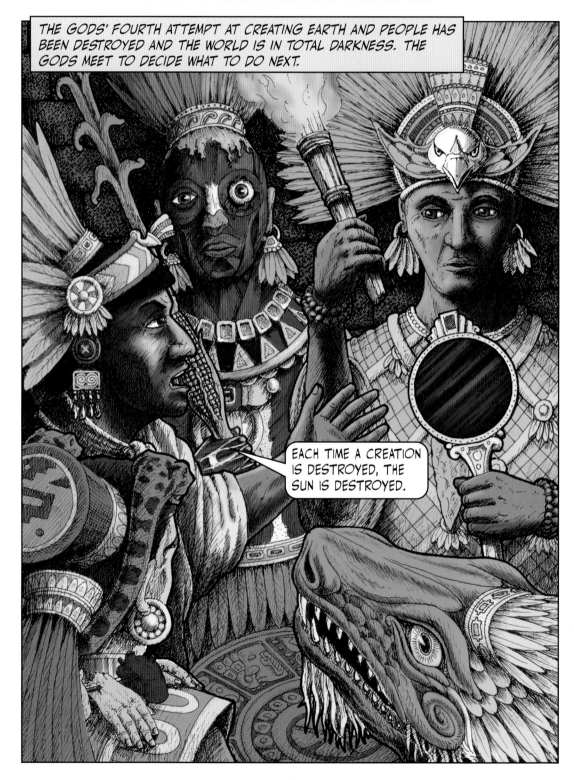

THE GODS' FOURTH ATTEMPT AT CREATING EARTH AND PEOPLE HAS BEEN DESTROYED AND THE WORLD IS IN TOTAL DARKNESS. THE GODS MEET TO DECIDE WHAT TO DO NEXT.

EACH TIME A CREATION IS DESTROYED, THE SUN IS DESTROYED.

ONE OF THE GODS MUST JUMP INTO THE FIRE TO CREATE A NEW SUN. WHO AMONG YOU WILL SACRIFICE YOURSELF?

TWO GODS STEP FORWARD. ONE IS RICH AND HANDSOME...

MY NAME IS TECCIZTÉCATL. I WILL JUMP INTO THE FLAMES AND BECOME THE MOST BEAUTIFUL AND BRILLIANT SUN.

THE OTHER IS POOR, UGLY, AND COVERED IN SORES.

I AM NANAUTZIN. I HAVE NOTHING TO OFFER YOU EXCEPT MY POOR BODY. BUT I WILL BECOME THE SUN IF YOU SO CHOOSE.

THE HANDSOME GOD IS GIVEN THE HONOR OF SACRIFICING HIMSELF. A FIRE IS PREPARED.

THE HANDSOME GOD IS ASHAMED OF HIS COWARDICE AND JUMPS INTO THE DYING FLAMES OF THE FIRE.

AT THIS POINT, A JAGUAR ALSO JUMPS INTO THE ASHES OF THE DYING FIRE.

WHEN IT LEAPS OUT, IT IS COVERED IN SOOTY PRINTS. THIS IS HOW THIS NOBLE BEAST GOT ITS MARKINGS.

THE GODS WATCH AND WAIT...

GRADUALLY, A GLOW APPEARS ON THE HORIZON...

SLOWLY, NANAUTZIN APPEARS AS THE SUN, RISING IN THE SKY...

BUT THERE IS SOMETHING NOT QUITE RIGHT...

...TECCIZTÉCATL, THE MOON, IS FOLLOWING THE SUN CLOSELY. HE IS SHINING JUST AS BRIGHTLY.

HOW DARE TECCIZTÉCATL DO THIS? HE DOES NOT DESERVE TO SHINE SO MUCH! ARRGGH!

THE ANGRY GODS SLAP HIM IN THE FACE WITH A RABBIT...

SCHLAPPP

AND THAT IS HOW THE MOON GOT ITS MARKS.

AFTER THE CREATION OF THE FIFTH SUN, QUETZALCÓATL DECIDED IT WAS TIME TO CREATE PEOPLE.

I SHALL GO TO THE UNDERWORLD AND ASK FOR THE BONES OF DEAD HUMANS FROM THE EARLIER CREATIONS.

BE WARY OF MICTLANTECUHTLI.*
HE IS NOT TO BE TRUSTED.

*LORD OF THE DEAD

MICTLANTECUHTLI GIVES QUETZALCÓATL A LARGE BAG FILLED WITH THE BONES OF DEAD PEOPLE.

I AM SURE I WILL SEE THEM AGAIN SOON ENOUGH. HA HA HA!

REMEMBERING THAT MICTLANTECUHTLI WAS NOT TO BE TRUSTED, QUETZALCÓATL RUSHES AWAY.

IN HIS HASTE, HE SLIPS AND DROPS THE BAG...

...BREAKING ALL THE BONES INTO SMALLER PIECES.

KERSNACK

LATER, ON EARTH, QUETZALCÓATL MIXES HIS BLOOD WITH THE BROKEN BONES TO MAKE THE PEOPLE OF THE FIFTH CREATION. ALL THE PIECES OF BONES ARE DIFFERENT SIZES. THIS IS WHY PEOPLE ARE DIFFERENT HEIGHTS AND SHAPES.

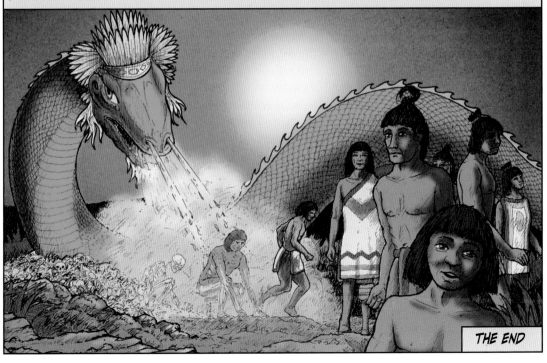

THE END

THE HERO TWINS
FROM THE MAYAN PEOPLE

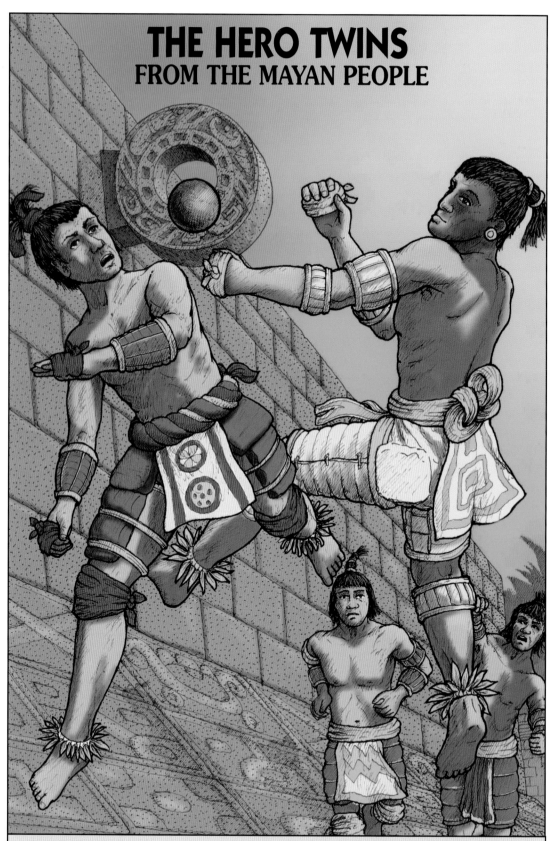

THE EARTH SHAKES AS THE BROTHERS HUN HUNAHPU AND VUCUB HUNAHPU PLAY BALL WITH HUN HUNAHPU'S SONS, HUN BATZ AND HUN CHOUEN.

HUN CAME AND VUCUB CAME ARE THE SUPREME GODS OF XIBALBA (THE UNDERWORLD). THEY ARE ANGRY.

WHAT IS THAT TERRIBLE NOISE? IS IT THOSE BROTHERS PLAYING BALL AGAIN? HAVE THEY NO RESPECT FOR THE GODS?

A MEETING IS CALLED. ALL THE GODS OF XIBALBA ARE PRESENT.

IT IS DECIDED! WE WILL CALL THE BROTHERS TO US. THEY WILL FAIL THE TASKS WE SET FOR THEM. THEN WE WILL KILL THEM AS A SACRIFICE.

ASK THEM TO BRING THEIR BALL-PLAYING GEAR. WE WILL WANT IT AFTER THEY ARE KILLED. SEND FOR THE OWL MESSENGERS.

THE OWL MESSENGERS, CHABI-TUCUR, HURACÁN-TUCUR, CAQUIX-TUCUR, AND HOLOM-TUCUR GIVE THE MESSAGE TO HUN HUNAHPU AND VUCUB HUNAHPU.

THE GODS OF XIBALBA DEMAND THAT YOU COME TO THEM WITH YOUR BALL-GAME GEAR.

LET US GO HOME TO SAY FAREWELL TO OUR FAMILY. THEN WE WILL COME WITH YOU.

THE TWO BROTHERS DECIDE TO HIDE THEIR GEAR IN THE RAFTERS OF THEIR HOUSE.

THEY WILL KILL YOU, MY SONS.

DO NOT WORRY, MOTHER. SEE, WE LEAVE OUR BALL-GEAR SO THAT WE CAN PLAY WHEN WE RETURN.

SOON, THEY ARE DESCENDING THE STEEP STEPS DOWN TO THE UNDERWORLD.

THEY CROSS MANY RIVERS AND PASS THROUGH MANY THORNY REGIONS WITHOUT HURTING THEMSELVES.

NEXT, THEY WALK THROUGH A RIVER OF BLOOD.

DON'T DRINK FROM IT! IT RUNS WITH BLOOD.

FINALLY, THEY COME TO A CROSSWAY.

I AM THE ROAD YOU MUST TAKE.

THE TWO BROTHERS FAIL THE FIRST TEST. THEY MISTAKE TWO WOODEN FIGURES FOR THE GODS.

HOW ARE YOU HUN CAME? HOW ARE YOU VUCUB CAME?

NEXT, THE GODS TRICK THE BROTHERS INTO SITTING ON A HOT BENCH. THEY FAIL THE SECOND TEST.

HA HA! TOMORROW, WE WILL PLAY A GAME OF BALL. TONIGHT, YOU WILL SPEND THE NIGHT IN THE HOUSE OF GLOOM. HERE ARE TWO CIGARS, AND PINE STICKS FOR LIGHT. YOU MUST RETURN THEM AS GOOD AS NEW IN THE MORNING.

HUN HUNAHPU AND VUCUB HUNAHPU SMOKE THE CIGARS AND BURN THE PINE STICKS FOR LIGHT.

IN THE MORNING, THE TWO BROTHERS COULD NOT RETURN THE CIGARS AND THE PINE STICKS AS GOOD AS NEW. THEY HAD FAILED THE THIRD TEST.

TODAY, YOU WILL DIE. YOU SHALL BE SACRIFICED!

THAT SAME DAY, THE BROTHERS ARE SACRIFICED. THEIR BODIES ARE BURIED UNDER THE BALL COURT IN XIBALBA.

THE HEAD OF HUN HUNAHPU IS CUT OFF AND PLACED AMONG THE BRANCHES OF A CALABASH TREE THAT HAS NEVER BLOSSOMED.

TO EVERYONE'S SURPRISE, THE TREE STARTS TO BEAR FRUIT. PEOPLE COME FROM MILES AROUND TO SEE IT. BUT THEY ARE FORBIDDEN BY THE LORDS TO PICK THE FRUIT.

ONE DAY, XQUIC, THE DAUGHTER OF LORD CUCHUMAQUIC, COMES TO SEE THE TREE.

I WONDER IF I CAN GET AWAY WITH PICKING SOME FRUIT?

THE SKULL OF HUN HUNAHPU APPEARS AND SPEAKS TO THE GIRL. AS SHE LIFTS UP HER HAND, HE SPITS INTO IT, MAKING HER PREGNANT WITH TWINS.

IF YOU WANT ONE, STRETCH OUT YOUR HAND. I WILL SPIT INTO IT, AND YOU WILL BE THE MOTHER OF MY CHILDREN.

WHEN IT IS DISCOVERED THAT XQUIC IS PREGNANT, HER FATHER TAKES THE MATTER TO HUN CAME AND VUCUB CAME.

VERY WELL. THE FOUR OWLS WILL TAKE HER TO BE SACRIFICED. THEY SHALL RETURN WITH HER HEART IN A GOURD.

THE OWLS SET OFF CARRYING A GOURD, A KNIFE, AND THE PREGNANT XQUIC.

OH! PLEASE! YOU CANNOT KILL ME. I AM PREGNANT WITH THE SONS OF HUN HUNAHPU.

WE DO NOT WANT TO KILL YOU, BUT WHAT CAN WE DO?

THEY DECIDE TO FOOL THE GODS BY MAKING A HEART FROM THE SAP OF THE RED TREE OF COCHINEAL.

PLACE THE "HEART" IN THE GOURD AND ADD SOME MORE RED SAP FOR BLOOD.

WE WILL RETURN TO YOU WHEN WE HAVE DELIVERED THIS.

THEY SHOW THE GODS OF XIBALBA THE FAKE HEART.

IT IS DONE. THROW IT ON THE FIRE!

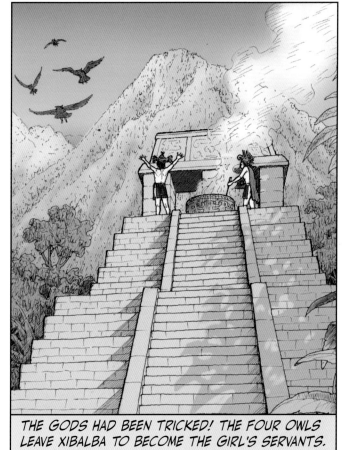

THE GODS HAD BEEN TRICKED! THE FOUR OWLS LEAVE XIBALBA TO BECOME THE GIRL'S SERVANTS.

28

XQUIC FINDS HUN HUNAHPU'S WIFE AND CHILDREN, HUN BATZ AND HUN CHOUEN, AND GIVES BIRTH TO THE HERO TWINS, HUNAHPU AND XBALANQUE.

HUN BATZ AND HUN CHOUEN BECOME JEALOUS OF THE TWINS. EVENTUALLY, THEY ARE TURNED INTO MONKEYS BY HUNAHPU AND XBALANQUE. BUT THAT IS ANOTHER STORY...

THE TWINS BECOME GREAT BLOWPIPE HUNTERS. BUT THEY DON'T DO ANYTHING TO HELP THEIR MOTHER OR GRANDMOTHER.

WHY DON'T YOU TWO FARM SOME LAND SO THAT WE MIGHT HAVE VEGETABLES TO EAT?

TO PLEASE THEIR MOTHER AND GRANDMOTHER, THE TWINS CLEAR A PATCH OF JUNGLE FOR FARMLAND.

THEY COME BACK THE NEXT DAY TO FIND THAT THE FIELD LOOKS LIKE A JUNGLE AGAIN.

WHO HAS DONE THIS?

I THINK IT WAS PROBABLY THE ANIMALS OF THE JUNGLE.

THEY CLEAR THE LAND AGAIN. BUT THIS TIME, THEY HIDE WHEN THEY HAVE FINISHED AND WAIT FOR DARKNESS.

AT MIDNIGHT, THE ANIMALS APPEAR IN THE AREA THAT THE TWINS HAVE CLEARED. THEY USE MAGIC TO MAKE THE TREES AND OTHER PLANTS GROW BACK AGAIN.

THE TWINS RUSH OUT TO GRAB THE ANIMALS, BUT MOST OF THEM ARE TOO QUICK. THEY CATCH THE TAILS OF RABBITS AND DEER, BUT THEY BREAK FREE, LEAVING THEIR TAILS IN THE TWINS' HANDS. THIS IS WHY DEER AND RABBITS HAVE SHORT TAILS.

EVENTUALLY, THEY CATCH A RAT. IT WILL NOT TALK TO THEM SO THEY HOLD ITS TAIL OVER A FIRE. THIS IS WHY RATS HAVE TAILS WITHOUT HAIR.

AAARGH! DON'T HURT ME!! YOU TWO AREN'T CUT OUT TO BE FARMERS. GIVE ME SOME FOOD, AND I WILL TELL YOU A SECRET.

THE RAT TELLS THEM THAT THEIR FATHER AND UNCLE WERE GREAT BALL-PLAYERS. HE SAYS THAT THE TWINS COULD BE GREAT PLAYERS, TOO, INSTEAD OF BEING FARMERS!

ALL YOU NEED IS SOME GOOD GEAR. AND I KNOW WHERE YOUR FATHER AND UNCLE HID IT.

THE RAT TAKES THEM TO THEIR GRANDMOTHER'S HOUSE AND POINTS TO THE RAFTERS.

THE TWINS TELL THEIR GRANDMOTHER TO GO OUT TO GET SOME WATER IN A JUG. THEY ASK A MOSQUITO TO MAKE A HOLE IN THE JUG. THEN THEY SEND THEIR MOTHER OUT TO FIND OUT WHY THEIR GRANDMOTHER IS TAKING SO LONG.

QUICK! NOW WE ARE ALONE! GET THE GEAR DOWN BEFORE THEY RETURN.

WE WILL HIDE IT IN THE FIELDS FOR NOW.

FOOD?

THE RAT GNAWS THROUGH THE ROPE AND THE SACK FALLS TO THE GROUND.

THE NEXT DAY, THE TWINS CLEAR THE BALL COURT THAT THEIR FATHER AND UNCLE PLAYED IN...

...AND BEGIN TO PLAY BALL.

WHO ARE THEY WHO SHOW NO RESPECT BY MAKING SUCH A NOISE? SEND FOR THEM. TELL THEM WE WISH TO PLAY BALL WITH THEM.

WHEN THE TWINS GET THE MESSAGE FROM THE GODS OF XIBALBA, THEY SAY GOODBYE TO THEIR MOTHER AND GRANDMOTHER.

THEY WILL KILL YOU LIKE THEY KILLED YOUR FATHER AND UNCLE.

DO NOT WORRY. WE WILL SUCCEED WHERE OUR FATHER AND UNCLE FAILED.

SOON THEY ARE DESCENDING THE STAIRS TO XIBALBA.

HAVING CROSSED MANY RAVINES, THEY COME TO THE RIVER OF CORRUPTION, WHERE THE PEOPLE OF XIBALBA HOPE THEY WILL FAIL.

DO NOT TOUCH THE WATER, BROTHER. DO AS I DO AND USE YOUR BLOWPIPE.

WHEN THEY REACH THE CROSSWAY, HUNAHPU PLUCKS A HAIR FROM HIS LEG TO MAKE A MOSQUITO.

XAN, GO AND STING THE GODS SO THAT WE WILL HEAR THEIR NAMES.

WHEN XAN STINGS THE WOODEN STATUES, THEY MAKE NO SOUND.

AH!

WHAT IS IT, HUN CAME?

AH!

WHAT IS IT, VUCUB CAME?

AH!

AH!

WHAT IS IT, AHALPUH?

WHAT IS IT,

THIS IS HOW THE TWINS LEARN ALL THE NAMES OF THE GODS OF XIBALBA.

AH!

AH!

THE TWINS IGNORE THE WOODEN STATUES AND GREET ALL THE GODS BY THEIR NAMES.

PLEASE TAKE A SEAT.

THEY DO NOT FALL FOR THE SECOND TRICK EITHER. THE LORDS OF XIBALBA ARE ANGRY. BUT THEY ARE SURE THAT THEY WILL FOOL THE BROTHERS IN THE NEXT TEST.

NOT ON THAT COOKING GRIDDLE WE WON'T.

THE PAIR ARE GIVEN CIGARS AND LIGHTED PINES AND ARE TOLD TO RETURN THEM IN THE MORNING.

TAKE THESE TO THE HOUSE OF GLOOM.

PUT OUT THE FIRE. WE CAN USE THIS MACAW FEATHER AS A FLAME. PUT A FIREFLY ON THE END OF YOUR CIGAR. THEY WILL THINK IT IS LIT UP.

FROM OUTSIDE, THE GUARDS ONLY SEE WHAT THE TWINS WISH THEM TO SEE.

WHAT TRICKERY IS THIS? NOW WE SHALL HAVE TO BEAT YOU AT BALL.

IN THE MORNING, THE CIGARS AND PINES ARE RETURNED WHOLE.

AND SO, THE TWINS PLAY BALL AGAINST THE LORDS OF XIBALBA, AND BEAT THEM BY SENDING THE BOUNCING BALL THROUGH THE STONE CIRCLE.

THE GODS ARE ANGRY AND GIVE THE TWINS ANOTHER SEEMINGLY IMPOSSIBLE TASK.

YOU SHALL SPEND THE NIGHT IN THE HOUSE OF KNIVES.

IN THE MORNING, YOU ARE TO GIVE US FLOWERS.

AT NIGHT, THE GUARDS DO NOT NOTICE THE ANTS STEALING THE FLOWERS IN FRONT OF THEM.

THE TWINS CONVINCE THE KNIVES THAT THEY SHOULD ONLY CUT THE FLESH OF ANIMALS.

THE TWINS THEN CALL THE ANTS TO THEM.

GO, ZOMPOPOS, AND CUT THE FLOWERS FOR US.

IN THE MORNING, THE TWINS PRESENT THE GODS WITH BUNCHES OF FLOWERS.

WHO ARE THESE PEOPLE? THEY HAVE TRICKED US AGAIN!

THE GODS PLAY WITH THEM AGAIN. THEY HOPE TO DEFEAT THE TWINS. SEVERAL GAMES ARE PLAYED, BUT ALL OF THEM END IN A TIE.

EVERY NIGHT, FOR THREE NIGHTS, THE TWINS ARE TESTED...

IN THE HOUSE OF COLD, THEY BUILD A FIRE TO KEEP WARM.

IN THE HOUSE OF JAGUARS, THEY FEED THE ANIMALS BONES.

IN THE HOUSE OF FIRE, THEY DO NOT BURN. ONLY THE WOOD BURNS.

THEN THEY ARE SENT TO THE HOUSE OF CAMAZOTZ, WHICH IS FULL OF BATS. BUT THE BROTHERS SLEEP INSIDE THEIR BLOWPIPES.

IS IT DAWN YET, BROTHER?

I WILL SEE...

IT'S...

SWISHHHH

AT DAWN, XBALANQUE FINDS HIS BROTHER'S DECAPITATED BODY. HE CALLS ALL THE ANIMALS TO BRING THEIR FOOD TO HIM.

AH, COATI. I WILL NEED YOUR SQUASH.

HE CARVES THE SQUASH TO LOOK LIKE THE HEAD OF HIS BROTHER.

XBALANQUE CALLS A RABBIT TO HIM.

HIDE BY THE BALL COURT NEAR THE TREE. WHEN YOU SEE THE BALL COME NEAR YOU RUN OUT INTO THE FOREST AS FAST AS YOU CAN.

THE GODS OF XIBALBA ARE SURE THEY WILL WIN. IN THIS FINAL GAME, THEY DECIDE TO PLAY WITH THE TWIN'S HEAD AS THE BALL.

XBALANQUE BOUNCES THE HEAD TOWARD THE TREE.

AS THE HEAD FALLS CLOSE TO THE RABBIT, HE JUMPS OUT AND HOPS INTO THE FOREST.

THERE IT GOES.

XBALANQUE REPLACES THE HEAD WITH THE SQUASH. HE HANDS HUNAHPU THE HEAD, AND HE PUTS IT BACK ONTO HIS NECK.

WATCH THIS!

THE GODS RETURN FROM THE FOREST AND SEE THE "HEAD" ON THE GROUND.

THERE IT IS!

HUH?

HAHA! HO! HO!

ONCE AGAIN, THE GODS OF XIBALBA HAVE BEEN OUTWITTED.

39

THE GODS OF XIBALBA CANNOT KILL THE TWINS, EVEN WITH ALL THEIR TRICKERY. BUT THE TWINS KNOW THEY CANNOT LEAVE UNTIL THEY ARE DEAD. THEY CALL THE WISE MEN TO THEM.

WHEN THE GODS OF XIBALBA ASK WHAT TO DO WITH US, TELL THEM TO CRUSH OUR BONES AND SPRINKLE THEM IN THE RIVER.

WHEN THE LORDS OF XIBALBA CALL THE TWINS TO A NEW GAME, THE TWINS KNOW IT IS A TRICK...

SEE THIS FIRE? WE BET YOU CAN'T JUMP OVER IT FOUR TIMES.

THEY BOTH JUMP INTO THE FIRE AND DIE.

THE LORDS OF XIBALBA ARE DELIGHTED THAT THE TWINS ARE FINALLY DEAD.

TELL US, WISE MEN, WHAT SHALL WE DO WITH THEIR BONES?

GRIND THEM UP AND THROW THEM INTO THE RIVER SO THAT THEY ARE SCATTERED FOREVER.

THE LORDS DO AS THE WISE MEN SUGGEST.

AS IT HAPPENS, THIS IS THE ONLY WAY THE TWINS COULD BE BROUGHT BACK TO LIFE. FIRST AS CATFISH...

...THEN AS MEN. BUT NOBODY RECOGNIZES THEM BECAUSE THEY LOOK LIKE BEGGARS.

THEY TRAVEL AROUND XIBALBA, ENTERTAINING THE PEOPLE WITH THEIR SONGS, DANCES, AND THEIR MAGIC. THEY CAN BURN A HOUSE DOWN AND THEN REBUILD IT IN A MOMENT. THEY CAN ALSO CHOP A MAN INTO PIECES AND THEN BRING HIM BACK TO LIFE.

WHEN THE LORDS OF XIBALBA HEAR OF THESE BEGGARS WHO CAN DO MAGIC, THEY HAVE THEM BROUGHT BEFORE THEM.

OH, MY LORD!

WE HAVE HEARD A LOT ABOUT YOUR MAGIC. SHOW US WHAT YOU CAN DO! KILL THAT MAN, AND THEN BRING HIM BACK TO LIFE.

SEE, HIS HEART NO LONGER BEATS.

AND NOW YOU SEE HE IS TRULY ALIVE.

OH, MY. WHAT HAPPENED? I FEEL WONDERFUL. JUST AS IF I HAVE BEEN REBORN.

YOU MUST DO IT TO US.

ME FIRST!

THE TWINS KILL BOTH HUN CAME AND VUCUB CAME. BUT THEY DO NOT BRING THEM BACK TO LIFE. AND SO THIS IS HOW THEY FINALLY DEFEAT THE GODS OF THE UNDERWORLD.

ALL POWER IS TAKEN FROM THE PEOPLE OF XIBALBA, AND THEY ARE REDUCED TO THE LOWEST RANK AND ARE NEVER ALLOWED TO PLAY BALL AGAIN. NEVER AGAIN WOULD THE KINGDOM OF XIBALBA BE GREAT.

WE ARE HUNAHPU AND XBALANQUE. WE ARE THE SONS OF HUN HUNAHPU.

THEY ARE TOLD OF THE RESTING PLACE OF THEIR FATHER AND UNCLE UNDER THE BALL COURT.

THEIR NAMES SHALL NEVER BE FORGOTTEN.

FINALLY, THE TWINS FLOAT INTO THE SKY TO BECOME THE SUN AND THE MOON.   **THE END**

43

MORE MYTHICAL CHARACTERS

There are thousands of characters in Mesoamerican mythology. They include gods and sacred animals, as well as human figures.

BACABS – The Bacabs are the four jaguar gods who hold up the sky. They also guard the four points of the Mayan compass. Each jaguar has its own color: north is white, south is yellow, west is black, and east is red. In Mayan mythology, the jaguar is a sacred creature.

CABRACA – Cabraca is an evil Mayan giant who is also called the Mountain Destroyer. He is killed by the Hero Twins, who tricked him into eating a poisoned wildfowl (a type of bird), and when he was too weak to defend himself, the twins buried him alive.

CAMAZOTZ – This Mayan god of darkness and caves is also known as Zotz or Zotzilaha Chimalman. He is a bat, and he cut off Hunahpu's head when Hunahpu and Xbalanque spent the night in the bat cave.

CINTEOTL – Cinteotl is the Aztec god of corn (maize), which is the staple diet of the Aztecs. He is often shown wearing a headdress made from ears of corn and is protected by Tlaloc.

COATLICUE – This Aztec goddess gave birth to the moon and stars. She is usually shown wearing a skirt of snakes woven together, and is known, in particular, as the mother of Huitzilopochtli.

EHÉCATL– Ehécatl is the Aztec god of wind. He brought romantic love into the world when he fell in love with Mayahuel, whom he took from the underworld. When Mayahuel died, Ehécatl planted her bones in the ground. Over time, they grew into a plant that produced white wine.

GUCUMATZ – Gucumatz is a Mayan creator god, known as Kukulkán by the Toltecs. He and Omecihuatl try many times to create people.

First they use mud, but these people wash away. Then they try wood, but these people do not have a soul. Eventually, they use maize, and this works.

HUITZILOPOCHTLI – This Aztec god of war is thought to be the sun reborn. Huitzilopochtli kills his brothers and sisters (the moon and the stars) as soon as he is born. The fight between them is seen as a fight between day and night. Each time morning comes, Aztecs believe that Huitzilopochtli has won again over the moon and stars.

HURACUN – An important Mayan creator god who is known as the god of storms. The English word "hurricane" comes from his name.

OMECIHUATL – Omecihuatl is the Aztec goddess of duality because she is two opposites, a man and a woman, at the same time. She gives birth to a stone knife and throws it at Earth to create 1,600 heroes. These heroes create the first people, with help from Xolotl.

TEPEU – A Mayan god of creation who made Earth and everything on it. He, with help from Gucumatz, created it many times because they were not pleased with what they had made.

TLALOC – Tlaloc is the Toltec and Aztec rain god. He is called Chac by the Mayans and rules an Aztec heaven for people who have drowned. He is worshipped because rain allows maize to grow.

XIUHTECUHTLI – This is the Aztec god of fire and time. He is often shown with a red or yellow face. A fire was lit inside the chest of a sacrificed victim once every fifty-two years in his honor.

XOCHIQUETZAL – Xochiquetzal is the goddess of love, beauty, dance, flowers, and women. Her name means "feather flower." Every year, a feast was held in honor of her at which people would wear animal and flower masks.

XOLOTL – An Aztec dog-shaped god, he went to the underworld to find bones of the first dead humans so he could create more people. Xolotl is Quetzalcóatl's twin brother.

GLOSSARY

arc The curve of the sun's passage across the sky during the day.

bear fruit When a plant blossoms to produce fruit.

blowpipe A tube used mainly for hunting. A hunter would insert a dart into the end of the pipe and blow into the opposite end sharply to fire out the dart.

calabash A thorny tree common in Mexico and Central America.

coati A type of racoon from Mexico and Central America.

corrupt Being deceitful.

crossway The point where two or more roads meet each other.

decapitated When someone has had his or her head cut off.

descendants People who can trace their roots from a particular individual or group.

divert To change the way in which something is traveling.

downfall When a civilization is defeated.

gourd A fruit with a hard shell, such as a pumpkin, that has been hollowed out and dried.

haste To do something quickly and in a hurry.

jaguar A big cat with a deep yellow coat marked with dark rings, spots, or rosettes.

macaw A type of parrot found in Central America.

outwit To win by the use of skill and cunning.

Popol Vuh A sacred book of the Mayan people.

rafters The beams that support a sloping roof.

rank A level of authority.

ravines Small, narrow tracks with very steep sides that have been created by water running quickly through them.

sacrifice When a person is killed to honor the gods.

sap A liquid that carries food and important substances inside a plant. It is often sticky, such as the sap from the maple tree that is eaten as maple syrup.

soot A black powder that is made by burning something.

tlachtli The sacred ball-game played by the Mesoamericans.

trickery Playing against another person unfairly, and cheating in order to win.

zompopos A leaf-cutting type of ant that is very common in Guatemala, Central America.

FOR MORE INFORMATION

ORGANIZATIONS

The Metropolitan Museum of Art
1000 Fifth Avenue
New York, New York 10028-0198
Phone: 212-535-7710
TTY: 212-650-2921
Web site http://www.metmuseum.org

Peabody Museum of Archaeology and Ethnology
Harvard University
11 Divinity Avenue
Cambridge, MA
Web site http://www.peabody.harvard.edu

FOR FURTHER READING

Bellingham, David, Margaret Carey, David Jones, Kathleen McPhilemy, and Louise Tythacott. *The Kingfisher Book of Mythology*. London, England: Kingfisher Publications Plc., 2001.

Bingham, Ann. *South and Mesoamerican Mythology A to Z*. New York, NY: Facts On File Inc., 2004.

Ferguson, Diane. *Tales of the Plumed Serpent: Aztec, Inca and Maya Myths*. New York, NY: Sterling Publishing Company, 2000.

Fisher, Leonard Everett. *Gods and Goddesses of the Ancient Maya*. New York, NY: Holiday House Inc.,1999.

Montejo, Victor, Luis Garay (Illustrator), and David Unger (Translator). *Popol Vuh: A Sacred Book of the Maya*. Ontario, Canada: Groundwood Books, 1999.

INDEX

Web Sites

Due to the changing nature of Internet links, the Rosen Publishing Group, Inc., has developed an online list of Web sites related to the subject of this book. This site is updated regularly. Please use this link to access the list:
http://www.rosenlinks.com/gm/meso